Praise Works!

Harnessing the Power of Praise, Worship &
Thanksgiving for a Victorious Life

"Let the people praise thee, O God…" Psalm 67:5

RALI MACAULAY

Other Books by Rali Macaulay

Scripture Works!

7 Days of Power

DEDICATION

To my Lord and Savior, Jesus Christ. I am grateful for your unfailing love and faithfulness that has brought me this far; and keeps me going. Thank you for choosing me for this assignment, and for the grace for completion.

To my husband, Ibukunoluwa. In so many ways, I have learnt the unfailing love of God through you. Thank you for believing in me, and for the gentle nudges along the journey of completing this book.

To my precious little children, Ara, Ini and Eri. You make life so meaningful, and I feel so blessed to be your mother. Love you all so much!

To my mother. Thank you for teaching me the virtues of discipline, hard work, and determination.

To my siblings, family and friends. You all have enriched my life with your friendship, support and prayers; and I'm blessed to have you all in my life.

Presented To:

_____

From:

_____

Date:_____

CONTENTS

Introduction   i

1. Praise, Worship & Thanksgiving   Pg 1
2. Grace Enabled Praise   Pg 10
3. Garment of Praise – Praise Prep   Pg 15
4. Praise, Your Spiritual Transaction   Pg 25
5. When Praise Becomes A Sacrifice   Pg 30
6. Weapon of Praise/Praise Warfare   Pg 38
7. Attitude of Gratitude   Pg 46
8. Praise Rewards   Pg 56
9. Praise Methods   Pg 73
10. Praise, A Way of Life   Pg 83
Salvation Prayer   Pg 90

Psalm 150

Praise ye the LORD. Praise God in his sanctuary: praise him in the firmament of his power.

Praise him for his mighty acts: praise him according to his excellent greatness.

Praise him with the sound of the trumpet: praise him with the psaltery and harp.

Praise him with the timbrel and dance: praise him with stringed instruments and organs.

Praise him upon the loud cymbals: praise him upon the high sounding cymbals.

Let every thing that hath breath praise the LORD. Praise ye the LORD.

INTRODUCTION

> *Let the people praise thee,*
> *O God; let all the people*
> *praise thee. Psalm 67:5*

Growing up, a common adage I heard often was "God does not eat physical food. Praise and thanksgiving are God's food" (translated). Another was, "Anyone that give thanks for today's goodness, will receive more goodness" (again translated).

One of the easiest things we can give to God is praise, worship and thanksgiving. A thankful heart will always have more to be thankful for. A grateful heart will be far from depression. A praiseful heart will always attract God's presence and glory. Praising God with a sincere heart will enhance your relationship and fellowship with God. It will fill your heart with love for God, and your fellow man. It will also position you above your circumstances. It will bring God himself into your affairs.

One of the things I enjoy doing is singing the praises of God. I remember back then, as a new young believer, sitting on our balcony with my little instrument, singing praises endlessly. Many times I would take my hymn book and just sang my heart out. I did this not fully aware of the benefits of praise as I am today; but because it was done in love, and sincerity of heart, the blessings of praising God were still unleashed in my life in ways I never could have comprehended!

In more recent times, as I began to better understand the power in praising God, I began to apply it to different situations. I discovered that praise will strengthen your relationship/fellowship with God. Praise can be used as a weapon of deliverance. It can be a medium of tapping into God's supernatural provision. In praise, you can secure God's heavenly protection. Likewise through praise and thanksgiving, you secure the blessings of

God in your life. With praise, you can get answers to long-standing questions of life. In short, praising God will give you victory in life. I have heard numerous testimonies of people who after having prayed about a situation for so long, decided to switch to praise; and it is amazing how things began to change for them even after they had stopped praying but were simply praising.

Praise truly is a powerful force. Indeed, Praise Works!

***

Even though praise is such a powerful tool in the believer's life, many have relegated it to a mere ceremony, something you do while waiting for other members of the church to congregate. Some would even wait until after the praise and worship section before they appear at church; and personal time of praise? Unfortunately many believers don't have one; maybe an occasional "thank you, Lord", or "praise the Lord", here and there but nothing frequent, nothing consistent. Any wonder we often feel weak, and discouraged?

If you knew the power of praise, I guarantee you; you would do it more often. Don't be deceived one more day! Praise is potent. It is of a truth one of the most powerful forces in life! Praise can turn impossible situations around. Praise will move the hands of God on your behalf. Praise will bring you the miraculous. Praise will drive out depression, it will give you hope and restore your joy. Whatever you face in life, you name it, praise will handle it.

Praise and thanksgiving is how we enter into God's presence, even in our prayer time. *"Enter into his gates with thanksgiving, and into his courts with praise: be thankful unto him, and bless his name." -Psalm 100:4.* Even the Lord Jesus himself started his prayers with praise and thanksgiving; and taught his disciples to pray same way in Matthew 6:9 *"After this manner therefore pray ye: Our Father which art in heaven, Hallowed be thy name."* We are also admonished to add thanksgiving to our requests (Philippians 4:6). In fact we should start and end our prayers with praise and thanksgiving.

The most incredible testimonies have been through the power of praise – check the testimony of the wall of Jericho falling down before the Israelites, as a result of their heart-felt praise, giving them unprecedented victory (Joshua 6:1-20). History has it that this wall was so thick; several horses could ride on it, side by side! Even Rahab's house was part of the city wall! (Joshua 2:15 (NIV)). That was how fortified it was, but praise brought it down. Praise is a spiritual dynamite! In the same way, praise is capable of bringing down every mountain on your path to getting to God's Promised Land for you. Your promise land may be marriage, it may be education, it may be a house, divine healing…whatever it is, your sincere praise of God is powerful enough to deliver it to you!

Testimonies abound, of people who praised their way out of barrenness to fruitfulness, after many years of childlessness. Some have praised their way to their God-ordained spouse. Yet others have testified of promotions and miraculous deliverances. It is endless, the blessings that come from praising God.

Personally, I recall a time I desperately needed to change jobs for better work/life balance. I prayed, fasted, sent my resumes in. I did everything I knew to do; but nothing seemed to be happening. Then, by the leading of the Holy Spirit, I started to praise him. Each evening, I'd keep my appointment with God, and just praised. I stopped asking; all I did was praise, worship and gave him thanks. It was amazing! Shortly after that I got a call from a place I didn't even remember applying to. The Lord moved so fast, that very shortly after that I got the job, and it became one of the best jobs I ever had. When you really think about it, if we believe he heard us when we prayed, then we should naturally make praise and thanksgiving our next move, shouldn't we? Just as someone aptly said, "Thanksgiving is your greatest expression of faith".

Praise still works! We may not have been engaging it much, but it does not stop the truth that praise will move God to arise on your behalf. Even today, we hear praise reports among believers, of victories gotten through praise. You can have your own praise report too...because Praise truly is a potent force.

The following pages will highlight in more details how God's power can be unleashed through our praise, worship, and giving of thanks. We will also look at the corresponding rewards and benefits of praise. Yes, when praise is done right, it comes with rewards, and brings God's blessings. This book will help you to better understand the power of praise; and how it ushers in God's presence and blessings into your life situations. You can secure your breakthroughs with your praise. There is power in praising God...put on your garment of praise, and let's go. Praise Works!

1. PRAISE, WORSHIP & THANKSGIVING

> *Enter into his gates with thanksgiving, and into his courts with praise: be thankful unto him, and bless his name.*
> **Psalm 100:4**

Oftentimes in Christian gatherings, when we mention praise, we automatically think of that part of the service where we sing fast songs, clap, dance, and even shout. Well, these are part of it, but not all there is to praise. In fact, praising God is way deeper than that.

It is in praise that we celebrate God for who he is. In praise, we adore him. In praise, we exalt his name. We express our love to him just because we love him. Praise is celebrating God for his unfailing faithfulness, and his loving kindness. In our praise we glorify our God; we lift him up and declare his greatness, his majesty, and his marvelous works to the children of men. *"Oh that men would praise the LORD for his goodness, and for his wonderful works to the children of men!" –Psalm 107:31.* Our praise also expresses our complete trust in God.

Praise is the vehicle that takes us out of the natural, into the realm of the Spirit; to experience God's supernatural presence and power. Praise enables us to experience and bask in God's glory.

Praising God will change your heart and fill you with love for God and others!

Worship is closely related to praise. We almost cannot differentiate one from the other; and definitely cannot separate the two. Worship is when we honor God as the Sovereign One; as the Almighty; as our Deity, the One that is above all, and supreme to all. In worship we magnify God. We ascribe greatness to our God; we recognize his divinity. We recognize and reference him as our Maker, our Creator, expressing our deep love for him. We can also worship God through our offerings and by serving him.

How about thanksgiving? This is how we appreciate God for his deeds in our lives, for what he has done and will do. We express our gratitude to him in our thanks. We acknowledge his goodness in our lives and thank him for all of his past deeds, as well as his promises to us, because we know that *"Faithful is He who calls you, and He also will bring it to pass." -1 Thessalonians 5:24 (NASB)*

As we can see, praise is not isolated. Praise, worship and thanksgiving are inter-related. As you worship God, you'll often see yourself constantly moving from praise to worship, and to thanksgiving; and back to praise. Don't fight it. Let it flow.

***

Although praising God is very important, it is even more important to give him acceptable praise. You may wonder at the use of the word "acceptable", but it is possible to "praise" God for long hours, and as loudly as we possibly can, but at the end only succeeded in giving him "lip service". *"These people honor me with their lips, but their hearts are far from me." –Matthew 15:8 (NLT).* It is not about the expression or the words we utter alone, it is also about connecting with him in our hearts, lifting him high, and shifting the atmosphere so much so that his glory descends, like it did with King Solomon in 2 Chronicles 7.

Praise is not what we do to while away the time, nor should it be done only when we are in church. No, in fact, we are called to praise not just at church, but in our private time of fellowship with God as well; which brings me to another point. When we praise God what is our motive? When we give him our dance in the congregation, raise our hands, shout his praise (especially when people are around us), what is our motive? Are we praising him in sincerity, or to impress those around us, and show them how spiritual we are?

There is absolutely nothing wrong with praising him selflessly in front of others, but we must be careful not to do so for the applause of men. On the other hand, we must also not let the presence of others inhibit our freedom in expressing our love to God in worship. We must approach him and worship him like it is just us and him, and no other soul present; whether we are in private or in the congregation.

David was a great example of a true worshiper. He gave his best dance before the Lord regardless of who was watching or what they thought of him. I love how he said in 2 Samuel 6:21 (paraphrased) "it is before the Lord that I danced". He was indeed a true worshiper. No wonder he was said to be a man after God's heart (Acts 13:22).

Our praise of God will help us shift our focus away from self, and from our problems, to the Most High God. That is why we have been admonished, to praise God, in all things; to give him thanks always! *"Give thanks in all circumstances; for this is God's will for you in Christ Jesus." -1 Thessalonians 5:18 (NIV)*

*When we praise
God, he does for us
what we cannot do
for ourselves.*

When we render acceptable praise to God, it gets his attention. God cannot be mocked. He searches and knows the intent of every heart. He asks that we worship Him in Spirit and in truth – *"God is a Spirit: and they that worship him must worship him in spirit and in truth". John 4:24.* No matter how much of the motions of praise we exhibit, if our hearts are not right before God, we have just merely been having a religious exercise. But sincere praise will touch God's heart and usher us into his presence and glory.

I believe your desire is that your praise be acceptable to God; that the time you spend in his presence be meaningful; and that you do not leave his presence empty. Know what? That is God's desire too. He wants to visit with you. He wants to fellowship with you. He wants to spend time with you, just like he did when he originally created man, before sin separated man from God. But thank God we have access to God again through Jesus Christ. So come boldly into his presence and offer him quality praise; and be rest assured that anytime you get in his presence, you will not leave empty. You will always leave better than you came.

Here are some of what happens when you praise God:

- Something changes inside of you for the better.

- Your spirit man is strengthened.

- You feel loved and confident.

- It drives away your fears.

•You have an assurance in God that you cannot explain.

These are just a few of the benefits of praise. We will examine some more later on in this book.

2. GRACE ENABLED PRAISE

> *For by grace are ye saved through faith; and that not of yourselves: it is the gift of God:*
> *Ephesians 2:8*

There is nothing we have that his grace did not provide; and there's nothing we are outside of God's enabling grace. *"But by the grace of God I am what I am, and his grace to me was not without effect. No, I worked harder than all of them-yet not I, but the grace of God that was with me."* -1 Corinthians 15:10 (NIV). Yes, we do our parts (like mentioned in this verse) because "faith without works is dead" –James 2:17; but without God, we can do nothing (John 15:5). It is God that keeps us alive today. It is he that gives the strength to do whatever we do. He woke us up this morning. He kept us save through the night. He provides the air that we breathe. Indeed without him we are nothing! It is by his grace that we are who and what we are. Thank you, Jesus!

***

When you understand grace, you will praise more spontaneously and more often. Grace extends God's love to us even when we don't deserve it. Grace brings God's goodness into our lives when we least feel worthy of it. Grace looks beyond us to the cross, to the shed blood of the Messiah, Jesus Christ; to the finished work Jesus did on the cross when he died for our sins. Grace shows us God's everlasting love for us, it reveals his preference for us; and helps us see ourselves, not only as we truly are, but as God sees us.

Understanding God's grace in our lives helps us love God more, and to extend the same grace and love to others.

Understanding
grace enhances
your worship of
God

When we remember that while we were yet sinners, Christ died for us (Romans 5:8); it moves us to a deeper appreciation of his grace. Like a songwriter put it, "I owed a debt I could not pay; he paid a debt he did not owe". Grace brought us salvation at such a great cost – God's only begotten Son! *"For the grace of God that bringeth salvation hath appeared to all men. Teaching us that, denying ungodliness and worldly lusts, we should live soberly, righteously, and godly, in this present world"* –Titus 2:11-12.

Understanding that grace will help us commit to a life of godliness and praise to him who chose us to be partakers of his grace.

The more our praises are propelled by our understanding of God's grace, the greater our ability to offer him true worship, as we realize how much his love has given to us already. Especially when we understand that he chose us, we cannot but be eternally grateful to him for counting us worthy of his love and grace. When you understand your adoption into God's Kingdom, that God had a choice of several others, but preferred you; that he chose YOU; you will naturally long to reciprocate such great love, and honor him in return.

***

You must know him to praise him. You cannot praise who you don't know. If you don't know God, or his works and deeds, praising him becomes tasking. Familiarize yourself with the works of God by spending time reading the bible. Meditate on God's word; there you will find several records of God's love, God's power, God's deeds, miracles, sovereignty, and majesty. The more you discover him, the more you will be equipped to praise him with understanding. Your grace-enabled praise springs from your experiencing and understanding God's grace. This experience humbles you, and leaves you in awe of him.

3. GARMENT OF PRAISE – PRAISE PREP

> *Let the words of my mouth, and the meditation of my heart, be acceptable in thy sight, O LORD, my strength, and my redeemer.*
>
> **Psalm 19:14**

How do we appear before the Lord to praise him? He has extended his hand of fellowship to us, but even then we must come before him with a pure heart, not "spiritually unkempt"; not with hearts full of bitterness, unrighteousness or any other form of sin.

The parable of the wedding banquet in Matthew 22 paints a very good picture for us. In this parable, the original guests gave excuses and did not attend the banquet. So the Master sent his servants to extend the invitation to others that normally did not qualify to be in the wedding feast. But guess what? One of these new invitees came not dressed right for the wedding (verse 12).

Notice that even though grace was extended to this individual, and he was invited to the wedding without being on the original guests list, it was still required of him to come appropriately dressed! In the same way, we must approach God's throne respectfully. We may have things that need to be taken care of, for our praises to ascend to God as sweet smelling savor.

To give God acceptable praise, here are some of the ways we can prepare:

Get Rid of Strife:

When we approach God in worship, we should come with no offense in our hearts against any. We must come before him with a pure conscience, forgiving anyone that may have offended us. *"Therefore if thou bring thy gift to the altar, and there rememberest that thy brother hath ought against thee; Leave there thy gift before the altar, and go thy way; first be reconciled to thy brother, and then come and offer thy gift."* -Matthew 5:23-24

"And when ye stand praying, forgive, if ye have ought against any: that your Father also which is in heaven may forgive you your trespasses." –Mark 11:25

Not only will strife hinder prayers, it will likewise stifle praise. You can't be sincerely praising God, and at the same time harboring anger or hatred against someone. In fact, if while you are praising, you remember any incidence or person that upsets you, quickly pray for them, forgive and release them from your heart. This will help free you up to give God quality praise.

Walk in Love:

Nothing works without love. We cannot give God true praise without love. We cannot praise who we don't know; and if we don't love, then we don't know God... *"Whoever does not love does not know God, because God is love." -1 John 4:8 (NIV)*.

Regardless of our gifts, or position in the church, without love, our service, and praise of God, will be meaningless (1 Corinthians 13:1-3). Love is the fulfillment of the law. (Romans 13:10). How can we offer sincere praise to him, and declare our love for him when we don't love our fellow men that he created? *'If anyone says, "I love God," and hates his brother, he is a liar; for he who does not love his brother whom he has seen cannot love God whom he has not seen.' -1 John 4:20 (ESV)*

If, for any reason, loving has been a challenge for you, ask God to fill your heart with his love, and he will. If we ask anything according to his will, he hears us (1 John

5:14); and loving others is definitely his will. *"You shall love the Lord your God with all your heart and with all your soul and with all your strength and with all your mind, and your neighbor as yourself." -* Luke 10:27 (ESV)

Also spend time meditating his love for you as recorded in the bible. The books of 1 John and the Psalms are good places to start. When you understand that you are his beloved, and that you are accepted by him, it becomes easy to not only embrace his love, but let it flow through you to others around you.

Praise, when done right, changes you!

Be Deliberate:

Come to praise God purposefully, determinedly, and excitedly. Don't come reluctantly. Remember he looks at the heart; we may fool man, but God can never be fooled. He knows the intent of every man's heart. Even days you are not in particularly high moods; still approach God's throne in sincerity of heart and reverence. He loves to fellowship with us. In fact we were created for his glory, to give him praise. *"Even every one that is called by my name: for I have created him for my glory, I have formed him; yea, I have made him." – Isaiah 43:7*

Coming before him purposefully will help you reap the blessings in worship.

Be Expectant:

When you worship him, do so expectantly. Expect him to receive your praise and worship. Expect him to speak to you. Expect there to be a spiritual exchange (a transaction, if you will) between you and him. In most cultures, you do not visit a king and leave empty. First you visit a king with a gift, but then as you leave he showers you with his own gifts, which most often will far outweigh what you offered him. When Sheba visited Solomon, she went with gifts (her offerings), but left with way more than she presented to the king (1 kings 10:1-13). Our praise is our offering as we approach the Most High God. It is our gift to him. There is no way he will let us leave empty if our worship is right, so be expectant.

Worship Him in Spirit and Truth:

That is certainly a requirement for acceptable praise. He sees your heart anyway, so why not just worship him with sincerity of heart. *"But the hour cometh, and now is, when the true worshippers shall worship the Father in spirit and in truth: for the Father seeketh such to worship him. God is a Spirit: and they that worship him must worship him in spirit and in truth." -John 4:23-24*

Worship has moved beyond just physical "tabernacles", to the hearts of men. That was why, when the Samaritan woman at the well spoke of worshiping on the mountain (John 4:20), Jesus brought her back to worshiping the Father in spirit and in truth. In other words, location is no longer important; we can worship God anywhere, and at anytime; not just at church or on Sundays. Worshiping in spirit and in truth is loving the Lord our God with all our hearts, all our souls and all our strength (Deuteronomy 6:5). It is being passionate about God and worshiping out of our love for him. It is knowing the God that we worship *"You worship what you do not know; we worship what we know, for salvation is from the Jews." -John 4:22 (ESV)*. This is one of the reasons why we must give the knowledge of God's word preeminence in our lives. The more we study God's word, the more we increase in our knowledge of him. That way, our worship can be based on the truth that we discover in his word.

Be Focused:

How many times have we started to praise God and found our thoughts wandering off! I can't tell you how many times I would be worshiping, and next moment, I'm planning my days schedule, or thinking through what needs to be done once I was done praising God! Once we become aware that we are getting off-course, go right back to focusing on God. Cast off any negative or distracting thoughts. *"Casting down imaginations, and every high thing that exalteth itself against the knowledge of God, and bringing into captivity every thought to the obedience of Christ;" -2 Corinthians 10:5*

I don't want to take God for granted. If I were having a conversation or fellowship with someone, and got distracted, what would I do? I'd apologize and get right back to giving them my attention. It's exactly same with the Lord. We shouldn't just jump back and forth. We should realize we do have an appointment with him at that time, and treat him with respect.

So when distracted, get right back to focusing on him. If closing your eyes help, then by all means, close it! Whatever you do, make the time you spend in his presence meaningful. Even if it's just few minutes, make it productive.

4. PRAISE: YOUR SPIRITUAL TRANSACTION

> ***Whoso offereth praise***
> ***glorifieth me: and to him that***
> ***ordereth his conversation***
> ***aright will I shew the salvation***
> ***of God. Psalm 50:23***

Do you know there's a transaction, an exchange, happening when we worship God? Many times we approach God's throne with our praises and worship, religiously utter the right words and raise our hands, without any expectation or understanding of what is happening in the spirit realm as we praise.

A while back, during a session of praise and worship with my family, I sensed the Holy Spirit teaching me that as we worshiped God, our praises ascend to heaven, as sweet smelling savor. But then it does not end there. As we send our praises up, God's blessings come down. In other words, when we give quality praise, there is an exchange between the earth and heaven. Something is leaving us, in exchange for something more glorious and far better, because it is coming from our Father in heaven, who we can never out-give! That is why when you worship, you get directions from God; he drops his instructions in your spirit. It could be a solution you have been seeking. It could be an idea that will propel you to your next level. It may be his peace. You may be exchanging your weaknesses for his strength. There is always a transaction going on as you praise him! Remember that!

When Praises Go Up, Blessings Come Down!

Never round up your worship thinking you are the only one that just "gave" something.

Not so. It's a two way transaction, if it has been done in spirit and in truth. You may not see any manifestations immediately, you may not even feel any special change occurring, but know that you are not leaving his presence empty.

When we appear before the Lord, we must come believing that he will receive our praise, worship and thanksgiving. We must believe he takes over our deepest needs, some of which we may not even be aware of, and in exchange gives us his best.

***

As we praise God, we exchange our defeat for his victory; our frustrations for hope in him. We hand him our pains and broken hearts, and receive his love and healing. When you praise God, and his glory descends, the devil and every evil spirits around you have no choice but to flee! Your burdens get lifted as you praise God, and you get his peace that passes men's understanding instead. *"Do not be anxious about anything, but in every situation, by*

27

prayer and petition, with thanksgiving, present your requests to God. And the peace of God, which transcends all understanding, will guard your hearts and your minds in Christ Jesus." (NIV) -Philippians 4:6-7.

Saturate your dwelling place with praise. Fill your hearts with constant thoughts of God's goodness, and praise. When you worship him, exchange every spirit of heaviness for the garment of praise; exchange your mourning for joy; your ashes for his beauty, as you praise, worship and give him thanks. *"To appoint unto them that mourn in Zion, to give unto them beauty for ashes, the oil of joy for mourning, the garment of praise for the spirit of heaviness; that they might be called trees of righteousness, the planting of the LORD, that he might be glorified." -Isaiah 61:3.*

Praise is a door opener! Your praise will open supernatural doors for you.

If you need direction for any issue in your life, your time of worship is a great time to ask the Lord. When you feel his presence so strong ask about any pressing issues you have needed answers to and the Spirit will guide you.

5. WHEN PRAISE BECOMES A SACRIFICE

> *Therefore, let us offer through Jesus a continual sacrifice of praise to God, proclaiming our allegiance to his name. Hebrews 13:15 (NLT)*

I had just received bad news that day. I dragged my suddenly "heavy" legs through the door, into my home. My husband was not home yet, the kids still at school. With very heavy heart, feeling like all strength was drained from me, I laid prostrate on the living room floor. That was all I could do at that moment. I couldn't even pray, not right then...and last thing I wanted to do was praise! Praise? Don't you need a joyful heart to praise? Mine was sorrowful right then. But then I knew better. Thank God for the several messages I had read and heard of God's unfailing love even when nothing seems to be working; messages of praising God in different situations. So right there on the floor, I pushed past the fear of tomorrow, past the dread of uncertainty and began to force out the words, one at a time… "Lord, I choose to trust you", "I praise you, Lord", "Thank You, Jesus". Yes these were not excited utterances, in fact they were mixed with tears, but they were much needed to destroy the wiles of the devil, right then. And the more I dwelt on God's faithfulness in the past, day after day, and began to find things to be grateful for, and focus on those things and his promises; it became easier to praise him with joy in my heart.

How about you? Have you ever not felt like praising God, no matter how hard you tried? Maybe you just got unpleasant news, like it happened in my case above. It could be that you just lost a loved one, a job, or a valuable asset. It may be that you just experienced a relationship breakup; or perhaps it's an evil report about your health. Whatever it was, it left you feeling emotionally drained, like in a battle that left you beaten and weary. It left you feeling angry, maybe. It may not even be something so serious, probably you're just a little disappointed - you didn't get the promotion again; or it could be that you are frustrated about an issue. Whatever it was, you were left feeling spiritually dry, and uninterested in worship. Sometimes, you may not even be able to pinpoint what it is, but you just aren't "feeling" it!

You see, even at those times when you are most vulnerable, God is waiting to hold you. He is right there with you, and more than ever, you need to worship him at such times. You must not rely on emotions or feelings when it comes to doing God's will and his will is that you praise him. Whatever is happening in and around you, praise is still comely. *"I will bless the LORD at all times: his praise shall continually be in my mouth." -Psalm 34:1*

When you least feel like praising God, that is when you need to praise him the most!

When you praise him at such times, regardless of what is happening, or how you are feeling; when you praise him when you really don't want to; you offer him a "Sacrifice of Praise". It is a choice you make - a choice to praise even though it makes no sense; a choice to trust in his goodness, and praise him still. When you really think about it, a sacrifice, simply put, is going out of your comfort zone to do something different from what you would rather do. It is giving up your own convenience, for the pursuit and achievement of a less desirable option at that moment. Let's face it, the natural tendency is to curl up and moan on days you're not feeling too great. The effortless act is to complain and see only all the things that have gone wrong; or are about to go wrong. That exactly is where the devil wants you! But turn the table on him; shake yourself free. Arise! Take hold of the word of God on his goodness, faithfulness, and unfailing love. Like Job declare, "Though he slay me, yet will I trust in him" Job 13:15. Because really, he is not slaying you. The enemy is bringing the attacks, so that your faith can fail (See Luke 22:31-32). But you will not fail when you choose to trust God, and turn to praise instead of complaints.

Praising God in the midst of problems is giving it all to him, trusting him with your problems and believing him for a better future. It is believing that all will be well and all things will work together for your good.

Deliberately recall his past acts of kindness and love to you, and give him some heartfelt, prison-shaking praise. That is your sacrifice of praise! When you don't feel like it, want to, or see why you should praise God, go ahead all the same and praise him for Who he is. Hallelujah! And the testimonies must flow in. You can praise yourself out of every valley of life!

There have been miraculous interventions recorded resulting from people praising God when they least felt like it. So never let your feelings dictate when you should fellowship with God. Make yourself praise him, regardless. In my story above, that period became one of the best times of my life, in terms of my relationship with God and other areas of my life. He filled me with peace and joy. He gave me supernatural wisdom that led to great increases. When you are down, praise God and he will lift you out of any pit you are in. He will crown you with glory and honor; for when he is lifted up, he draws men unto him. *"And I, if I be lifted up from the earth, will draw all men unto me." -John 12:32.* Lift him up in your praise; and since he is above all, the only way he is drawing you is upwards. Rejoice!

Your sacrifice of praise will also bring you deliverance like it did for Jonah. Right in the belly of the fish, Jonah prayed in the earlier verses of Jonah chapter 2. But then he switched to a sacrifice of praise in verse 9 *"But I will sacrifice unto thee with the voice of thanksgiving; I will pay that that I have vowed. Salvation is of the Lord."* And the result was deliverance as God intervened in Jonah 2:10 *"And the Lord spake unto the fish, and it vomited out Jonah upon the dry land".* Your praise of God has the power to bring you out of that pit!

Are there things you believe God for? Start to praise him for them now. Praise him even before you see any manifestation of your expectation. Praise him because you believe, and are holding fast to your profession of faith: *"Let us hold fast the profession of our faith without wavering; (for he is faithful that promised;)"* - *Hebrews 10:23*. Even though we have not seen it, yet we praise him still. Our praises at this time will invite his intervention, and bring him into our situations and circumstances.

I pray your sacrifice of praise will turn into amazing testimonies too, in the name of Jesus.

6. WEAPON OF PRAISE/PRAISE WARFARE

> *Let the high praises of God be in their mouth, and a twoedged sword in their hand; Psalm 149:6*

Praise is a powerful weapon of warfare! It can never lose a battle. It is one of the most effective weapons available to the believer. When you praise God, the enemy shivers. Your praise incapacities and disarms the devil. It renders him completely powerless. As you praise God, his glory descends with his power, and no evil force can withstand God's power. *"Tremble, thou earth, at the presence of the Lord, at the presence of the God of Jacob;"* -Psalm 114:7

Praise Warfare:

Your battle is when you refuse to give up, and instead committing to fighting the good fight of faith (1 Timothy 6:12). How? You begin to praise God in the very situation that's bringing you pain and concern. Not praising him for bringing it your way, because he did not bring sorrow your way. He is a loving Father. *"And remember, when you are being tempted, do not say, "God is tempting me. "God is never tempted to do wrong, and he never tempts anyone else." —James 1:13 (NLT).* Center your praise on his promises concerning that situation. Your praising him in that situation is an expression of your faith in those promises of God to you. Give him a mountain-moving praise, that is praise that refuses to give up until God's intervention is manifested.

Praise will never lose a battle!

When the battle is toughest, when it looks like all hope is lost and nothing good is possible, give him praise. *"And at midnight Paul and Silas prayed, and sang praises unto God"* –*Acts 16:25*. When you have done all else and nothing seem to be happening, switch to praise. When you sense the presence of evil around you, praise, praise and praise again. Turn on your worship music and give him some praise dance. Saturate your environment with praise and worship music. That is your battle, your fight of faith; your praise warfare!

The devil can never stand the presence and power of God released through praise and worship. In Acts 16:26 we read *"And suddenly there was a great earthquake, so that the foundations of the prison were shaken: and immediately all the doors were opened, and every one's bands were loosed."* That is how powerful praises are. It answers with speed, and opens closed doors, when you get involved in true high praises of God. Praises will release the breakthrough anointing on your life! Your praise warfare is capable of uprooting every plantation of evil in your life.

If witnessing the manifestation of God's

promises in your life has been a challenge; if you are constantly being attacked by the evil one, then begin to praise God more than you've ever done before. Get into deep praise and worship; give him some earth-shaking praise like Paul and Silas did. As you do so, your praise releases the power of God and binds the enemy, destroying every yoke on your life. It stops your enemies, and brings God's judgment on your adversaries. *"Out of the mouth of babes and sucklings hast thou ordained strength because of thine enemies, that thou mightest still the enemy and the avenger." -Psalm 8:2.* Your praise will silence the enemy. The more you praise him, the greater your victory. Don't ever stop praising. Don't be weary in well doing (Galatians 6:9).

***

Praise changes the battle from being yours to God's. When Jehoshaphat and the people of Judah and Jerusalem worshipped God in 2 Chronicles 20, God took over their battles in such a way that the other kingdoms around them became afraid of God, when they heard how he defeated the enemies of God's people. Notice the way this battle was conducted:

First, they heard God's promise: *Jahaziel said, "Listen to me King Jehoshaphat and everyone living in Judah and Jerusalem! The Lord says this to you: 'Don't be afraid or worry about this large army, because the battle is not your battle. It is God's battle! -2 Chronicles 20:15 (ERV).* Same way God has promised us today, in several places in his word, that we have victory in Jesus. We have a part to play in that we need to believe God's word to us. It is our faith in his word that will help us move to the next phase recorded in this story.

They believed and praised God extravagantly: *Jehoshaphat bowed with his face to the ground. And all the people of Judah and Jerusalem bowed down before the Lord and worshiped him. The Levites from the Kohath family groups and the Korah family stood up to praise the Lord, the God of Israel. They sang very loudly. -2 Chronicles 20:18-19 (ERV).* They praised God because they believed the word they received. Do you believe the word the Lord is bringing you in that situation? If you do, then it's time to let that faith move you to give him quality praise like it's already done!

Next day, they praised some more: *Jehoshaphat encouraged the men and gave them instructions. Then he had the Temple singers stand up in their special clothes to praise the Lord. They marched in front of the army and sang, "Give thanks to the Lord! His faithful love will last forever." -2 Chronicles 20:21 (ERV).* Know what that tells us? It's not a one day faith thing, and then back to fear, doubt and unbelief. No we must keep believing, even if the situation looks like nothing is changing. Also notice they did not run from the battle, they were instructed to go to the battle (verse 16).

Someone has said, what you don't confront, you cannot conquer. Running from your problems will not take them away. You must seek God and receive instructions on how to conquer them. Also notice that they put praise first! Hallelujah! The singers matched before the armies! What an interesting picture. They were going to battle, but then the choir went first, the armies with the physical weapons of war were behind. That tells me the spiritual weapons are far more effective than the physical! *"The weapons we fight with are not the weapons of the world. On the contrary, they have divine power to demolish strongholds."* 2 Corinthians 10:4 (NIV)

And they saw results, while still praising: *As they began to sing and to praise God, the Lord set an ambush for the army from Ammon, Moab, and Mount Seir who had come to attack Judah. The enemy was defeated! The Ammonites and the Moabites started to fight the men from Mount Seir. After they killed them, the Ammonites and Moabites turned on themselves and killed each other. -2 Chronicles 20:22-23 (ERV).*

It didn't end there either: *Jehoshaphat and his army came to take things from the bodies. They found many animals, riches, clothes, and other valuable things. It was more than Jehoshaphat and his men could carry away. There was so much that they spent three days taking everything from the dead bodies. -2 Chronicles 20:25.* They didn't only defeat the enemy without the physical stress of a battle, but the Lord gave them spoils to take with them. The Lord will not only fight your battles as you praise him, but he will also shower you with so much blessings that you will be amazed!

After the battle they had honor: God was glorified and feared by their enemies; and they enjoyed the peace of God (verse 29). That is the power of praise used in battle. Whatever you have been battling, hand it over to God today through your praise.

7. ATTITUDE OF GRATITUDE

> *And whatsoever ye do in word or deed, do all in the name of the Lord Jesus, giving thanks to God and the Father by him. Colossians 3:17*

Gratitude is being thankful, being appreciative of a good done to you. When we express gratitude for what a person does for us, they tend to be willing to do much more. Same is true with God. When we are grateful for what he has done, is doing, or has promised to do, he blesses us even more. Know that whatever you are thankful for, will multiply. Complaining on the other hand will draw in more reasons to complain. So desist from complaining. Praising and complaining don't go together! One brings in more blessings (Praise), the other drives blessings afar (Complaints). In fact complaining can even attract curses like it did when the Israelites complained. The bible called it "murmur"; some translations use the word "grumble". *"Neither murmur ye, as some of them also murmured, and were destroyed of the destroyer."* - *1 Corinthians 10:10.* As we can see in this verse, complaining opens the door to the destroyer. We shall not be destroyed, in the name of Jesus.

Watch what is coming out of your month. More importantly watch what you're feeding your mind. *"A good man out of the good treasure of his heart bringeth forth that which is good; and an evil man out of the evil treasure of his heart bringeth forth that which is evil: for of the abundance of the heart his mouth speaketh" Luke 6:45.* Just like many Christians have trained their spirit and mind against cussing, we should equally train ourselves against complaining. Instead, when that negative situation creeps into your life, combat it with praises of what God has done in the past, and what you believe he will yet do again. *"Whoso keepeth his mouth and his tongue keepeth his soul from troubles." -Proverbs 21:23.*

Expressing gratitude is one of the greatest ways to turn things around in your life. If you gave a gift to someone who never expressed gratitude, would you be excited to give to them next time? Probably not. Like the proverb says, "Giving to an ungrateful person is like being robbed". If gratitude is that important to us, why do we think it is okay to only complain to God? Why don't we practice what we would like others to do to us with God? *"Do to others whatever you would like them to do to you. This is the essence of all that is taught in the law and the prophets". -Matthew 7:12*

*A grateful heart
is a thankful
heart*

People murmur and complain for many reasons. Many times what triggers murmuring is looking at the things that are not yet happening but which we so much desire to have or see in our lives. Other times dissatisfaction and murmuring are the result of comparing ourselves with others. The Bible says when we do that, we are not wise! (2 Corinthians 10:12). We unconsciously make them our standard, and so hinder ourselves from seeing and appreciating what God has already done for us. We are so focused on what we feel he has not done, that we forget to count our blessings and see the marvelous things he's already done.

One of the reasons gratitude is important is that it fills you with joy, and you need to praise God with a joyful heart for your praise to be acceptable. Your joyful expression of praise counts. Remember God loves a cheerful giver.

Gratitude makes you joyful, and joyfulness helps you to be praiseful.

Developing an attitude of gratitude as a life style, a way of life, benefits you immensely. For one thing, it brings you peace of mind and contentment. Praise and thankfulness is one sure way to battle anxieties, depression and sorrow. Taking time to be appreciative of what and who you have, lifts you out of sadness, and fills you with love and joy instead. Develop an attitude of gratitude. Look for what to be grateful for in EVERY situation. There is always something to thank God for if you take the time to examine your life. You cannot be a person of praise, and be depressed at the same time. It's just not possible.

I encourage you to take the **"Gratitude Challenge"** at the end of this chapter.

Gratitude List:

"Praise the LORD, my soul, and forget not all his benefits--Psalm 103:2

What are the things you are grateful for? I love to call them "My Thankfuls" I encourage you to take this exercise. List what you are grateful for. The things and people in your life right now that you take for granted, imagine life without them. How would that feel? You have eyes to read this, how will life be without those eyes? Unimaginable, right? Yet we take such things for granted. Purpose in your heart to be thankful. Use the "**Gratitude Prompts**" below to start building your list of what you are thankful for. I call them the "**Gratitude List**". Of course, come up with new ones to add to your list. The more you think about this exercise, the more things you'll find to be thankful for.

***

Deliberately shift your thoughts from complaints to that of gratitude. Because, really, whatever you keep dwelling on is what continues to be your life experience. Some called it the law of attraction, what you focus on the most, you attract. We see it in the bible as *"For as he thinketh in his heart, so is he:…"* - *Proverbs 23:7*. So choose to dwell on the good, the praise-worthy; and you'll consequently experience more of such.

The more things you realize you have on your Gratitude List, the greater the peace of God you'll experience. Your joy will begin to build up, and your trust will grow, knowing that he who did these things in the past, will do it yet again.

Gratitude Prompts:

- If you're reading this right now, be thankful you have eyes to read, and can read
- Do you hear noises around you? Then thank God you can hear.
- Have a roof over your head? Then lift your voice in praise of his name.
- Be thankful for the life he has given you, it's a gift you know? When there is life, there is hope.
- Do you have food to eat? Don't forget to say "Thank You, Lord"
- Appreciate God for the people in your life –family and friends…and yes for those

who sometimes give you headaches, because know what? You may actually miss them if they left your life

There is joy in gratitude

Gratitude Challenge

Take the Challenge:

- **Challenge 1:** Be thankful, and not complain for a whole day! Find what to thank God for all through the day. Can you do that? Let's try it.
- **Challenge 2:** Let's take it further and do one straight week of zero complaints, grumbling or murmuring! Replace it with praise and thanksgiving.
- **Challenge 3:** Next is the 21 days challenge. Do 21 Days of no complaints, but rather giving of thanks.

Trust me, you are going to have many opportunities to not do this, but remember, *"I can do all things through Christ which strengtheneth me." Philippians 4:13.* Make a quality decision to do this. Send yourself a reminder every morning, and several times during the day. It could be something as simple as "Praise Challenge"; "Praise Alert"; whatever you want to call it. When you get that alert; take a pause and think of at least one thing to be grateful for, and praise him for it. And watch the miracles begin to roll in!

Choose to be thankful, and BE thankful.

8. PRAISE REWARDS

> *Let the people praise thee, O*
> *God; let all the people praise*
> *thee. Then shall the earth*
> *yield her increase; and God,*
> *even our own God, shall bless*
> *us. -Psalm 67:5-6*

First off, I want to be quick to reiterate that our primary purpose of praising God should not be to get things from him. We must praise him because he is God, and for whom he is in our lives. However, we must also not be ignorant that we cannot give to him without him reciprocating. Our praise glorifies God, but at the same time benefits us! I love to say

"You can't out-give God". He is the most generous Giver, and already gave us the Ultimate Gift - his only begotten Son, Jesus Christ. We must also remember he has promised, with him, to also freely give us all things (Romans 8:32). That is why we must be expectant in our time of praise and worship. God still works wonders through praise.

When we praise God, certain things naturally happen, but if we are not sensitive to the Spirit, we may miss them and not tap into these blessings.

When you praise, you receive grace for whatever you are going through.

Some of the things that occur when we praise, worship and give thanks to God are further explained below.

What Happens When we Praise God:

Below are some of the things that happen when we offer sincere praise, worship and thanksgiving to God. The list below is in no way exhaustive.

1. Your love for, and appreciation of, God increases

Praise makes your heart tender. As you think about the love and faithfulness of God in your life, it makes you more passionate about him. The more you reflect on the good he has done in your life, the more appreciative you are of him; and the more your love for him increases.

2. God's Divine Presence and Glory are released

When you praise God in spirit and in truth, you usher in his divine presence. *"But thou art holy, O thou that inhabitest the praises of Israel"* - *Psalm 22:3*. God inhabits our praise. Simply put, he dwells in, resides, lives inside of our praise. In other words when you give God quality praise, his presence engulfs you; and with his presence comes his glory.

As you praise him, he comes down into your situation and circumstances himself. When you pray, he sends his angels (Daniel 10:12), and devils may delay them as it happened with Daniel's prayer (Daniel 10:13). But when you praise him, he himself comes down in his glory and majesty, and tell me what devil can withstand the Almighty God? No evil can stand the presence of God. Hallelujah!

In Acts 16:26 we read, *"And suddenly there was a great earthquake, so that the foundations of the prison were shaken: and immediately all the doors*

were opened, and every one's bands were loosed."
When The Lord came into the prison, "IMMEDIATELY" their chains were broken! Your praise will bring God into your situation faster than anything else. There will be suddenness in the turning around of your situation, an immediate response to your condition! That is the power of genuine praise! Praise will loose you from any captivity.

3. Divine Deliverance

Still on the story of Paul and Silas, we see how their chains were supernaturally broken. The jailer almost killed himself fearing they had escaped (Acts 16:27); meaning they could have if they wanted to. Your true praise of God will bring you divine deliverance. When you praise him with understanding of God's power to deliver, and with the expectation that he will deliver you, you cannot but experience his deliverance; both spiritually and physically. In fact, even when you are unaware of your need for deliverance, his divine presence, which no evil power can withstand, will force there to be a deliverance wrought in your life! That is the power of true praise.

Paul and Silas praised him in their prison, They may have been mocked by those that heard them, but they praised all the same and they got their deliverance! Whatever prison you may be in today, you can praise your way out, in the name of Jesus. Praise will break any barrier. Praise will bring you out of any valley of life. It brings God into your particular situation, to bring you his great deliverance. Praise has the ability to release you from every form of bondage. May you be loosed from every bondage, in Jesus' name.

Praise will take you into God's presence, and drive out any evil around you!

Praise will even bring you salvation. The Jailer and his household (in the story of Paul and Silas) were saved as a result of the wonders experienced through praise. Praise also has the power to cancel every, and any, appointment with death (like we see in the same story of Paul and Silas), because Jesus is life, and your praise brings him into your life.

God and the devil can never cohabit. The more you praise God, the more his presence drives away evil from you! When light comes, darkness flees. When you praise, God comes in, so every demon must disappear. King Saul's case is a good example of this. Whenever Saul was possessed by an evil spirit, and David played his harp (in praise of God), the tormenting spirit would leave Saul (1 Samuel 16:23). See why it is important to saturate your personal life with praises of God?

4. Supernatural Victory

Praising God will bring you unexplainable, but undeniable victories. It will do what is humanly deemed impossible. How do you logically explain a people walking round a wall six days and the wall crumbling on the seventh day, at the shout of the people? (Joshua 6:20). Note that this is no ordinary wall. It is so thick and so strong that the harlot Rahab's house was built into it! *"So she let them down by a rope through the window, for the house she lived in was part of the city wall." -Joshua 2:15 (NIV).* That sure is not your everyday wall! But praise leveled it!

When you face situations that needs supernatural intervention, and you have prayed and done all else you know to do, devote yourself to engaging some time in high praises. 2 Chronicles 20:1-20 is also another demonstration of victory wrought by the power of praise. See chapter 6 for more on this.

5. Divine Direction

Because praise ushers in the glory of God, it puts you in a spiritually sensitive mode, where you are able to hear his voice more clearly and more distinctively. If you have needed direction concerning any issue, and not getting clarity; start to praise and worship. As his glory descends (you will know, because the spirit in you will bear witness to it); ask him for that guidance you need, and move back to praising him. Remember anything not done in faith is sin (Romans 14:23). Believe to hear his voice. He will drop the answers in your spirit.

Several times during my time of praise and worship, I have received instructions, directions and even ideas. Many times things that looked complicated suddenly receive clarity as I worship. Even when I was not particularly thinking of the situation right then, the Lord will just drop it in my spirit, and what looked so difficult suddenly gets a solution! What a blessing!

During Praise and Worship, your spirit tunes in to God's Spirit. In a way, it is the unifying of your Spirit with his. You are in God's presence where you can receive his plans and directions for your life. Your praise will bring you into realms of divine wisdom and empower you for exploits as you go past seeing your own abilities, to embracing God's ability. It is always a good practice to have something to write with handy when you praise God. This way, you can quickly jot down whatever instructions or directions he gives you during your time of worship.

6. Divine Restoration

Praise also has the ability to restore whatever the devil has stolen from you. For example, praise will restore your joy - it will drive away negative emotions of depression, hopelessness and the likes. It will restore your peace. Anything that's been broken in your live can be fixed in the place of praising God; because as you praise, God begins to move things around for you, and in your favor. His angels begin to work at the commandment of God to fix the broken pieces of your life.

Paul and Silas' experience caused them to be restored to honor and dignity (Acts 16:33-40). As you sow your praises and honor God, you also reap honor from men. God gives you his wisdom and anoint you for excellence, such that others around you will notice your uniqueness, and glorify God in you.

7. God Takes Over Your Battles

"For we wrestle not against flesh and blood, but against principalities, against powers, against the rulers of the darkness of this world, against spiritual wickedness in high places." -Ephesians 6:12.

Praise is a powerful weapon in battle. When faced with situations that you humanly cannot confront, praise God. When you feel the attack of the enemy on your life, move into high praises, and watch God confuse the enemy. As you praise God, he takes over your battles; and when he takes over, then the battle is over! He wins! Hallelujah!

I love reading about the battle in 2 Chronicles 20. The Israelites had prayed, their enemies were mightier than they, their hearts fainted in dread; and there seemed no way out for them...but then they switched over to praise! Read this in the bible and see how God confused their enemy and took over the battle. The Israelites won without even having to raise a finger in battle...all they did was raise their hands and voices up in worship of God - that sure is less stressful than going physically to do battle, wouldn't you say?

I once heard someone describe what happens when you praise and dance before God, so beautifully, that I chose never to forget it. I'll share it with you...

Imagine you are in a wrestling ring (which spiritually we are. We are constantly in a fight with the enemy for our God ordained purposes, and victories). However, the opponent is too strong for you. But you have a partner, God. As you are being beaten, you struggle to rise back on your feet. Eventually you are able to run to the side where your partner is eagerly waiting for you to tap him, so he can come into the ring to fight the opponent. You tap him, he comes in, you rush out, and since he is mightier than the opponent, he knocks him out, and YOU WIN!!! He did not just win, you BOTH win! Here's how praise works in battle: Your praising him, and dancing before him, right in the midst of that problem, is the way you "tap" God's hands, and get out of the ring, so he can step in and take over the battle! And since he cannot lose, then you win! Hallelujah!

You battle is not over until God takes over! Praise hands it over to God.

8. Fresh Anointing

Praising God brings fresh anointing. You need freshness in the spirit every day. You need fresh anointing for each day's battles, whether you're aware of it or not. *"For the weapons of our warfare are not carnal, but mighty through God to the pulling down of strong holds"* 2 Corinthians 10:4

You cannot be in his presence and his anointing not be deposited in you, if you believe for it. So believe and expect it.

"I have found David my servant; and with my holy oil have I anointed him" –Psalm 89:20. God's fresh oil will give you joy and great gladness.

9. Divine Joy and Strength

"Then he said unto them, Go your way, eat the fat, and drink the sweet, and send portions unto them for whom nothing is prepared: for this day is holy unto our Lord: neither be ye sorry; for the joy of the LORD is your strength." -Nehemiah 8:10

Praising God will fill you with joy unspeakable, because in his presence is fullness of joy (Psalm 16:11). Praise brings you comfort enabling you to face whatever challenges are on your part. In other words, your praise of God will strengthen your spirit man. It will mature you beyond being tossed about by every problem of life. When you live a lifestyle of praise, what unsettles others will not unsettle you. Your praise in all situations shows your confidence in God's love which translates to the strengthening of your faith. If you have been feeling down and discouraged lately, start to praise God, and your strength will be renewed. In your praise you empty your weakness, so you can be filled with his strength.

10. Divine Healing

He is the resurrection and the life. There is power in God's presence and glory, and this power is mighty enough to bring you divine healing. His power is able to resurrect any dead part of your body, if you believe and praise him with that understanding and expectation. Praise and thanksgiving rose Lazarus who was dead for four days (John 11:41-43); and no, that didn't happen just because it was Jesus, he said we will do greater works than he did, if we believe (John 14:12).

There are testimonies today of such great happenings! I actually heard of such testimony recently, brought about by faith in the power of God released through praise. God does not change, and his power can never diminish. What he did in bible times, he is still doing today, if we dare to believe him.

In addition to all the above, praising God also brings God's blessings and increased prosperity. *"Let the people praise thee, O God; let all the people praise thee. Then shall the earth yield her increase; and God, even our own God, shall bless us."* *-Psalm 67:5-6* When we praise him, he blesses us, and causes the earth to yield its increase unto us; meaning whatever we do as our livelihood will be blessed and bring us financial increase.

9. PRAISE METHODS

> *"God is a Spirit: and they that worship him must worship him in spirit and in truth." -John 4:24.*

There is no one way to praise God; and it is not necessary to get systematic about it. What is necessary, though, is to be led by the Spirit when you bring your praise before the Almighty God. We must not make the mistake of thinking we praise God only when we sing. Praise is way more than that. In fact, praise should be a way of life for every believer.

Here are some of the different ways we can praise God. However, I want to add that first and foremost our lives must be living sacrifices, holy and acceptable unto him.

We praise God in these ways, and more:

Singing:

"Let us come before his presence with thanksgiving, and make a joyful noise unto him with psalms. - Psalm 95:2. This is the most known method of praising God; and actually the only method many attribute to praise. This is when we sing songs of praises, glorifying his name and praising him for who he is, what he has done, or will do in our lives. You can either sing familiar songs, play music and sing along, or even compose yours out of the gratitude of your heart, and the leading of the Holy Spirit...sometimes songs you may not even remember later! However, singing alone, without a joyful heart, and when not done in

spirit and in truth, is nothing but mere entertainment. We must engage our hearts and seek to connect with our heavenly Father in our praises.

Lifting Holy Hands:

"Lift up your hands in the sanctuary and praise the LORD." -Psalm 134:2 (NIV) As we praise God, it is not out of place to lift up holy hands in worship. Lifting your hands to the Lord is, in essence, showing that you surrender to his lordship over your life. It is also a sign that you surrender your ability in exchange for his. It is like when a little child wants an adult to lift him up, he raises his hands up. As you raise your hands up to the Lord, lifting his name up, he in turn lifts you up, through promotions, advancements, breakthroughs, peace and so on.

> *Praise is a lifter.*
> *The more you*
> *praise, the more*
> *you're lifted!*

Dancing:

"Let them praise his name in the dance: let them sing praises unto him with the timbrel and harp" -Psalm 149:3. Another way we praise God is through our dance. We honor and entertain him with our dance. We express our submission to him by our dance. It is showing that we are surrendered enough to praise him unashamedly. David did this (2 Samuel 6:14). He praised him so much in the dance that he broke every "official protocol" expected of a king. But he was unashamed to praise God this way. We should be bold about our love

for God, and not be ashamed to express our reverence for him in our dance.

When God is praised in the dance, it opens the way for signs and wonders. Dance unto the Lord, Dance in secret, dance in the congregation. When you feel led to, dance. Don't let anything, or anyone, distract you. If you're sick, you can praise your way into your healing. If you can't dance fully, move whatever you can in your body. Paul and Silas were bound, but they still praised. No matter the sickness holding you bound, praise, force your way through and give him praise, and believe God for your healing. There is miracle power in praise!

Clapping:

When we clap, cheer, or applaud, we acknowledge a person's achievement or greatness. It is very much in place and scriptural to praise God by clapping our hands in our appreciation of him *"O clap your hands, all ye people; shout unto God with the voice of triumph." -Psalm 47:1*

Remember we also read that *"…Blessed be the LORD my strength, which teacheth my hands to war, and my fingers to fight:" Psalm 144:1.* As we praise him with our claps, we allow him to do spiritual warfare on our behalf. We may be unaware of this, but praising him in our claps is also a form of spiritual warfare, and because we are on the Lord's side, we win!

Making a Joyful Noise unto the Lord (Shouting):

"Make a joyful noise unto the LORD all the earth; make a joyful noise, and rejoice, and sing praise." – Psalm 98:4

Have you ever watched a soccer game before? What happens when your team kicks the ball into the opponent's goal-post? There is a shout of victory. I wouldn't call myself a die-hard soccer fan, but I do remember the long stretched-out shout of victory..."It's a Goal!!!!!" When we praise God with a shout, we acknowledge he is Supreme; he is matchless, he is the winner, he is the best, and he has our devotion. We celebrate him with great joy.

Praising him with a shout is another way we lift him up. *"God has ascended amid shouts of joy, the LORD amid the sounding of trumpets." -Psalm 47:5 (NIV)*. God steps in, goes in to defend you when you shout; it breaks every barrier, every "wall of Jericho" in your life. This was the final step that brought the wall of Jericho crumbling down *"So the people shouted, and priests blew the trumpets; and when the people heard the sound of the trumpet, the people shouted with a great shout and the wall fell down flat, so that the people went up into the city, every man straight ahead, and they took the city." -Joshua 6:20 (NASB)*. Praising God with your shout of triumph still has the same impact today. It gives you victory! We have almost become too sophisticated to shout, but it shouldn't be. We should shout his glory in our private time of worship, as well as when we are gathered together with the brethren to worship him. Don't be uncomfortable to give him shouts of praise, remember there is plenty of noise in heaven (Revelation 19:1)

Playing Instruments:

This is another way we can worship God. If you know how to, playing instruments are great ways to spend time praising God, and bringing his presence down. Even if you are not skilled in any technical instrument, simple instruments like the tambourine, maracas etc are also great to use in making a joyful noise unto the Lord. Just like mentioned earlier playing instruments in praise of God has been known to drive demons out of possessed people.

With Your Voice:

There is power in our words. Never eliminate expression in words from your praise and worship. Praise God for his greatness with your voice.

In Quietness:

There are moments when all you can do is just be still before the Lord. *"Be still and know that I am God...Psalm 46:10.* At such times, don't try to do more, if that is all you are being led to do. Just maintain your quietness before the Lord in worship and humble reverence of him.

Kneeling, Laying Prostrate, Bowing Down:

These are other ways we can be moved to praise and worship God. If you are drawn to kneel, lay prostrate, or bow your knees as you worship, do so. *"Come, let us worship and bow*

down. Let us kneel before the Lord our maker" –
Psalm 95:6 (NLT)

Extraordinary praise will usher in extraordinary testimonies

In Your Understanding and In the Holy Ghost:

You can praise him in your understanding, whether in English or any other language you speak. You can also praise him in the Holy Ghost, speaking in unknown tongues, as the Holy Spirit gives you utterance.

10. PRAISE - A WAY OF LIFE

> *I will bless the LORD at all times: his praise shall continually be in my mouth." -Psalm 34:1*

We must know him to praise him. In other words, we must have a relationship with him to be able to give him praise that touches his heart. Therefore, trusting Jesus as our Lord and Savior is a first step to living a lifestyle of praise; as he already told us, *"...without me ye can do nothing" (John 15:5)*. Also we cannot have access to God except through the blood of his Son, Jesus Christ. He is the Way (John 14:6). So if you are yet to make that commitment, you can do so today, right now. Pray the "Salvation Prayer" at the end of this book.

Addicted to Praising God (Praise Addict):

Seven times a day do I praise thee because of thy righteous judgments. —Psalm 119:164

In a good way, we should be praise addicts. Being a praise addict means we are always and continuously praising God; thanking him for every aspect of our lives. We should be quick to always give glory to God for everything he has given and made us; even for breathing, and being alive. *"Only the living can praise you as I do today. Each generation tells of your faithfulness to the next." -Isaiah 38:19.*

This life in itself is a gift. It is a privilege to be alive, so praise him even if you are still trusting him for many other things. Where there is life, there is hope, and our God is a master at turning around situations overnight!

He has done it many times before, and is still doing so today. Praise the Lord!

How do we become praise addicts? We make a conscious effort to be one. We look for opportunities to give him thanks and praise all through each day; we will find many reasons to praise him if we consciously consider this.

Cultivating a lifestyle of praise will preserve God's blessings in your life, and keep the door open for more of his blessings. It will make the joy of the Lord in you increase, and leave no room for depression. Ask God to restore the joy of salvation in your life (Psalm 51:12), and give that joy room to express itself. Dwell on things that are good, that are true, and are of a good report (Philippians 4:8)

If you are a praise-addict, you will be a mountain-mover. Never stop praising him. From your waking hours to night time, praise God. A life of praise is based on an absolute trust in God, that regardless of what is happening, or not happening, God is still good! A life of praise will keep you bubbling with the joy of the Lord.

In Praise of God:

Give him praise, worship and thanksgiving RIGHT NOW!

- Eternal Rock of Ages, I bless your name
- Lord, you are my God, and there is no other besides you
- I exalt and glorify your holy name
- You are the I am that I am
- Lord Jesus, I adore you
- I magnify your holy name
- You are the Mighty Man of War
- You are our soon coming King
- You are the Beginning and the End
- You are the Lily of the valley
- The bright and morning Sun

- The First and the Last

- The One that cannot fail

- The Most High God

- You are the everlasting King of glory

- You are the uncreated Creator

- You are the unchangeable Changer

- You are the God that is higher than the Highest

- You are light and in you is no darkness at all

- You are my King, my Redeemer, my Hope, my all in all.

Here are some verses on Praise from the Bible:
Let the saints be joyful in glory: let them sing aloud upon their beds. –Psalm 149:5

O praise the LORD, all ye nations: praise him, all ye people. –Psalm 117:1

Speaking to yourselves in psalms and hymns and spiritual songs, singing and making melody in your heart to the Lord; - Ephesians 5:19

Come, let us sing to the LORD! Let us shout joyfully to the Rock of our salvation. – Psalm 95:1 (NLT)

Therefore I will give thanks unto thee, O LORD, among the heathen, and I will sing praises unto thy name. -2 Samuel 22:50

It is a good thing to give thanks unto the Lord, and to sing praises unto thy name, O Most High: - Psalm 92:1

But thanks be to God, which giveth us the victory through our Lord Jesus Christ. -1 Corinthians 15:57

SALVATION PRAYER

For what shall it profit a man, if he shall gain the whole world, and lose his own soul? – Mark 8:36

If we confess our sins, he is faithful and just to forgive us our sins, and to cleanse us from all unrighteousness. 1 John 1:9

Neither is there salvation in any other: for there is none other name under heaven given among men, whereby we must be saved. –Acts 4:12

For whosoever shall call upon the name of the Lord shall be saved. Romans 10:13

Prayer:
Heavenly Father, I come to you this day, confessing my sins. I believe in the death and resurrection of Jesus Christ; I thank you for the provision you have made for me to be

saved through the blood of your son, Jesus. I believe your word that says whosoever shall call upon the name of the Lord shall be saved. Lord Jesus, I call on you to save and reconcile me back to God. I renounce my sins, and I confess that I believe that Jesus Christ is the Son of God. Right now, I accept Jesus as my Lord and Savior.

Lord Jesus, come into my life, and live your life through me. Fill me with your Holy Spirit and give me the grace to live for you all the days of my life. I thank you Lord for saving me. In Jesus' name I pray. Amen.

Notes

Notes

Notes

Printed in the USA
CPSIA information can be obtained
at www.ICGtesting.com
LVHW011327031023
760005LV00008B/270